SPEAK SOFTLY,
AND CARRY A
BEAGLE

SPEAK SOFTLY, AND CARRY A BEAGLE

by Charles M. Schulz

An Owl Book
Henry Holt and Company / New York

Henry Holt and Company, Inc.
Publishers since 1866
115 West 18th Street
New York, New York 10011

Henry Holt ® is a registered
trademark of Henry Holt and Company, Inc.

Library of Congress Catalog Card Number: 90-81564

ISBN 0-8050-1484-5 (An Owl Book: pbk.)

Henry Holt books are available for special promotions
and premiums. For details contact: Director, Special Markets.

First published in book form in 1975 under the same title
by Holt, Rinehart and Winston,

First Owl Book Edition—1990

Printed in the United States of America
All first editions are printed on acid-free paper.∞

3   5   7   9   10   8   6   4

Dear Contributor,

We think your new story is magnificent.

We want to print it in our next issue, and will pay you One Thousand dollars.

P.S. April Fool!

Dutch Waltz, the famous skater, was worried.

His skating partner, Chil Blain, was in love.

While playing a show in Denver, she had become involved with a cowboy named Martin Gale.

THE STORY ISN'T MUCH, BUT THE NAMES ARE GREAT!

"DEAR CONTRIBUTOR, YOUR STORY WAS TERRIBLE!"

"WE WOULD LIKE TO SEND IT BACK TO YOU, BUT YOU DID NOT INCLUDE RETURN POSTAGE"

"P.S. DON'T SEND THE RETURN POSTAGE NOW..."

"WE THREW YOUR STORY OUT THE WINDOW!"

Immediately after he won the golf tournament, he was interviewed on TV.

"This is the most exciting moment of my life!" he said.

"I saw you on TV," said his wife. "I thought the day we got married was the most exciting moment of your life."

In his next tournament, he failed to make the cut.

"DEAR CONTRIBUTOR"

"THANK YOU FOR SUBMITTING YOUR STORY TO OUR MAGAZINE"

"TO SAVE TIME, WE ARE ENCLOSING TWO REJECTION SLIPS..."

"...ONE FOR THIS STORY AND ONE FOR THE NEXT STORY YOU SEND US!"

Joe Anthro was an authority on Egyptian and Babylonian culture.

His greatest accomplishment, however, was his famous work on the Throat culture.

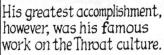

THAT'S THE DUMBEST THING EVER WRITTEN!

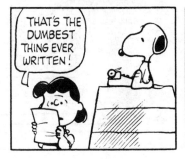

ANOTHER FIRST!

WOODSTOCK ALWAYS LIKES THE PART WHERE RHETT BUTLER WALKS OUT ON SCARLETT...

HI, CHUCK... IT'S BEEN KIND OF A LONG TIME, HUH?

YEAH, I'M BACK IN SCHOOL AGAIN...HOW'S SNOOPY'S DOG HOUSE? THAT SURE WAS EMBARRASSING...I HAD NO IDEA HE WAS A BEAGLE...

I USED TO THINK HE WAS JUST A FUNNY-LOOKING KID WITH A BIG NOSE...THAT'S WHY I HAVEN'T CALLED YOU, I GUESS....

LET'S JUST SAY MY PRIDE HAD THE FLU, OKAY, CHUCK?

EDUCATION IS IMPORTANT, FRANKLIN

SAY, FOR INSTANCE, THAT I'M THE MANAGER OF A MAJOR-LEAGUE BALL CLUB AND I'M TAKING THE LINEUP OUT TO THE UMPIRE...

THAT LINEUP HAS TO BE PUNCTUATED CORRECTLY, DOESN'T IT? YOU CAN'T TAKE A STARTING LINEUP OUT TO THE UMPIRE IF IT ISN'T PUNCTUATED CORRECTLY, CAN YOU?

EDUCATION IS IMPORTANT, FRANKLIN!

RATS!

HE WHO LIVES BY THE LOB DIES BY THE LOB!

OUT ?!!

BAD CALL!

IT HIT THE EXACT MIDDLE OF THE OUTER PART OF THE EDGE OF THE FRONT PART OF THE BACK PART OF THE LINE!

WE'RE THE HOME TEAM, CHUCK, SO YOU GUYS BAT FIRST, AND WE'LL TAKE THE FIELD..

OKAY, SNOOPY, YOU'RE OUR LEAD-OFF BATTER...LET'S START THINGS OFF BIG...

BUT LOOK OUT FOR PEPPERMINT PATTY...SHE'S A GOOD PITCHER!

HERE WE GO! THE FIRST PITCH OF THE SEASON! I LOVE BASEBALL!

BONK!!

WHAT KIND OF A GAME ARE YOU PLAYING?! YOU BEANED MY BEST PLAYER!

I DIDN'T DO IT ON PURPOSE, CHUCK...HE WAS CROWDING THE PLATE...I WAS JUST TRYING TO BRUSH HIM BACK!

FORGET IT! I'M TAKING MY TEAM HOME!

YOU CAN'T FORFEIT THE GAME, CHUCK!

IF YOU GO HOME, YOU LOSE! DON'T FORFEIT THE GAME, CHUCK!

I'M DISGRACED! WINNING A GAME FROM CHUCK'S TEAM BY FORFEIT IS THE MOST DEGRADING THING THAT CAN HAPPEN TO A MANAGER!

MAYBE YOU COULD FORFEIT THE FORFEIT, SIR..

STOP CALLING ME "SIR"!

I HAVE TO STAND OUT HERE ALL DAY, DON'T I?

I FIGURE IF I CAN TAKE CARE OF A FEW SHEEP WHILE I'M STANDING OUT HERE, I CAN PICK UP SOME EXTRA MONEY

TEAM OWNERS HATE TO SEE THEIR PLAYERS PICK UP SOME EXTRA MONEY!

DID WE REALLY LOSE THIS GAME OR WAS IT MY IMAGINATION?

IT WASN'T YOUR IMAGINATION... WE LOST FORTY-TO-NOTHING!

THEY GOT FORTY GOALS?!

THEY DIDN'T GET ANY GOALS... THEY GOT FORTY RUNS!

HOW COULD THEY WIN IF THEY DIDN'T GET ANY GOALS?

Our magazine assumes no responsibility for unsolicited material.

No such material will be returned unless submitted with a self-addressed envelope and sufficient postage.

U.S. MAIL

THEY PROBABLY DON'T REALLY MEAN IT!

Gentlemen,
    I am submitting a story to your magazine for consideration.

I have been a subscriber to your magazine for many years.

If you don't publish my story, I am going to cancel my subscription.

So there, too!

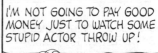

History Report;
Ancient Greece

Ancient Greece was ahead of its time, and before our time.

They had no TV, but they had lots of philosophers.

I, personally, would not want to sit all evening watching a philosopher.

MY GRANDFATHER HAS A BIRTHDAY THIS WEEK

DOES HE MIND GETTING OLD?

NO, HE SAYS IT DOESN'T BOTHER HIM... IN FACT, HE SAYS HE FEELS GREAT...

HE SAYS THAT ONCE YOU'RE OVER THE HILL, YOU BEGIN TO PICK UP SPEED!

HOW DO YOU LIKE THE SHOW SO FAR?

IT'S PRETTY GOOD, I GUESS..

DO YOU COME TO THESE SHOWS VERY OFTEN?

NO, THIS IS MY FIRST TIME..

ACTUALLY, THE MAIN REASON I'M HERE IS TO REVIEW THE SHOW FOR OUR SCHOOL NEWSPAPER...

SCHULZ

"THERE'S NO REASON FOR YOU TO KEEP COMING BACK TO THE NEST ON MOTHER'S DAY...THAT'S NOT THE WAY WE BIRDS DO THINGS!"

"ONCE YOU'VE LEFT, LITTLE BIRD, THAT'S IT! YOU CAN'T GO HOME AGAIN! SO FLY AWAY! DON'T LOOK BACK! THE WORLD IS YOURS!"

* SIGH *

I MUST ADMIT SHE'S A PRETTY SHARP MOTHER!

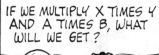

...WHO IS CRABBIEST OF US ALL?

I HAVE A QUESTION..

I'M WATCHING TV!

DO YOU THINK I'M CRABBY?

OF COURSE! YOU'RE PROBABLY THE MOST CRABBY PERSON THE WORLD HAS EVER KNOWN!

SOME PEOPLE ARE UP ONE DAY AND DOWN THE NEXT...YOU NEVER KNOW HOW TO TAKE THEM...YOU WOULDN'T WANT ME TO BE LIKE THAT, WOULD YOU?

AND WHO CAN BE PLEASANT ALL THE TIME? NO ONE CAN BE PLEASANT ALL THE TIME... WHAT DO YOU EXPECT OF ME?

I DON'T EXPECT ANYTHING OF YOU

YOU'RE NO HELP AT ALL!

ALL RIGHT, HOW ABOUT THIS? HOW ABOUT A YEAR'S SCHEDULE WHICH GIVES YOU TWO HUNDRED PLEASANT DAYS, ONE HUNDRED "REALLY UP" DAYS, SIXTY CRABBY DAYS AND FIVE "REALLY DOWN" DAYS? I COULD LIVE WITH THAT, I THINK...

CAN WE CALL TODAY ONE OF THE "REALLY DOWN" DAYS?

SURE.. WHY NOT?

POW!!

THIS IS GOING TO BE GREAT.. I STILL HAVE FOUR "REALLY DOWN" DAYS LEFT, AND I HAVEN'T EVEN TOUCHED MY SIXTY CRABBY DAYS...

SCHULZ

HERE'S THE WORLD-FAMOUS BEAGLE SCOUT SETTING OFF ON A HIKE..

HE TAKES WITH HIM ONLY THE BARE NECESSITIES...

EXTRA SOCKS, FIRST-AID KIT, A MAP, A COMPASS...

..AND LUNCH!

AN OBSERVANT SCOUT CAN LEARN A LOT ON A HIKE...

HE CAN LEARN ABOUT THE "WEB OF NATURE"

SUNLIGHT, AIR, PLANTS, WATER, SOIL, BIRDS, MICROORGANISMS....

ALL WORKING TOGETHER TO MAKE A BETTER LIFE FOR BEAGLES!

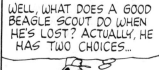

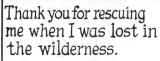

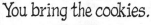

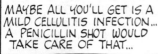

IF YOU'RE GOING TO HAVE YOUR EARS PIERCED, SIR, WHY DON'T YOU GO TO A DOCTOR?

HE'LL USE A HYPODERMIC NEEDLE, AND THEN, TO AVOID INFECTION, HE'LL PUT TWENTY-FOUR KARAT GOLD BARS IN YOUR EARS FOR TEN DAYS UNTIL THEY HEAL

HOW MUCH WILL HE CHARGE?

PROBABLY TWENTY DOLLARS...THAT'S THE COST OF AN ORDINARY OFFICE CALL

TWENTY DOLLARS?!! FOR TWENTY DOLLARS HE SHOULD PIERCE YOUR EARS, CHECK YOUR EYES AND CURE YOUR ASTHMA!

THE NURSE SAID THEY'LL PIERCE OUR EARS IF WE GET PARENTAL PERMISSION

THAT'S NO PROBLEM..

Dear Doctor,
Okay! Let her have her dumb ears pierced! I am sick and tired of arguing with her.

What can I do? Let her learn the hard way! What do I care? Go ahead! Pierce her dumb ears!

THAT'S PERFECT, LUCILLE! IT SOUNDS EXACTLY LIKE A FED-UP MOTHER!

Kitten Kaboodle was a lazy cat. Actually, all cats are lazy.

Kitten Kaboodle was also ugly, stupid and completely useless.

But, let's face it, aren't all cats ugly, stupid and completely useless?

I LOVE WRITING ANTI-CAT STORIES!

And so, once again, Kitten Kaboodle had to admit she had been outsmarted by a dog.

An ordinary dog at that.

DO YOU THINK THERE'S A MARKET FOR ANTI-CAT STORIES?

"PLAYBEAGLE" HAS BOUGHT THE WHOLE SERIES!

Secretly, Kitten Kaboodle wished she were a dog.

She was aware of the natural superiority of a dog, and it bothered her.

I THINK YOUR ANTI-CAT STORIES SHOW TOO MUCH PREJUDICE...I THINK YOU'RE GOING TO MAKE A LOT OF ENEMIES...

NOT EVERYONE HATES CATS, YOU KNOW!

I FIND THAT HARD TO BELIEVE

After that, Kitten Kaboodle never again tried to match wits with a dog.

DO YOU THINK YOUR ANTI-CAT STORIES WILL EVER BE MADE INTO A TELEVISION SERIES?

I EXPECT TO HEAR FROM ALL THREE NETWORKS... CBS, NBC AND ABC...

COLUMBIA BEAGLE SYSTEM, NATIONAL BEAGLE COMPANY, AND THE AMERICAN BEAGLE COMPANY!

PITCH IT TO 'IM, BOY!

THROW IT RIGHT PAST HIM!!

POW!

GUESS WHAT, MANAGER...ONE OF YOUR SOCKS FLEW CLEAR OUT TO THE CENTER-FIELD FENCE!

THAT MUST BE SOME KIND OF RECORD...WOULD YOU CALL IT THE LONGEST SOCK EVER HIT, OR JUST THE LONGEST SOCK? OR MAYBE YOU COULD CALL IT THE LONGEST SOCK EVER SOCKED...

HOW ABOUT THE LONGEST HIT EVER SOCKED OR THE LONGEST SOCK EVER SOCKERED?

WHY DON'T YOU JUST GET BACK IN CENTER FIELD WHERE YOU BELONG?!!

THIS IS THAT TIME OF YEAR WHEN BASEBALL MANAGERS ALWAYS START GETTING CRABBY!

SCHULZ

RATS!

I WOULD HAVE WON, BUT I GOT OFF TO A BAD FINISH!

POW!

HE WHO LIVES BY THE POACH DIES BY THE POACH!

I Never Promised You an Apple Orchard

YOUR STORIES HAVE NO FEELING!

WHY DON'T YOU WRITE A STORY WHERE A BOY MEETS A GIRL, THEN LOSES HER AND THEN WINS HER?

DO YOU WANT ME TO HELP YOU WITH YOUR STORIES?

! THAT'S A GOOD IDEA... I'LL JUST CLIMB UP HERE, AND HELP YOU...

THERE NOW... THIS IS GOING TO WORK OUT FINE... I CAN JUST SIT HERE AND WATCH WHAT YOU WRITE, AND GIVE YOU INSTANT CRITICISM...

WELL, GO AHEAD AND WRITE!! WRITE JUST WHAT YOU FEEL!

Bug off!

"GREETINGS! THIS IS TO INFORM YOU THAT YOUR APPLICATION FOR NOT GOING TO CAMP HAS BEEN TURNED DOWN..."

"THEREFORE, YOU WILL REPORT TO THE BUS TERMINAL AT 0800 TOMORROW WHERE YOU WILL BE TRANSPORTED TO CAMP TO SERVE A TERM OF TWO WEEKS"

WHY ME?

SO HERE I AM AT THE BUS STATION WAITING TO BE TAKEN TO CAMP...

HOW DO THESE THINGS HAPPEN TO ME? NO ONE ELSE I KNOW IS GOING...

MAYBE I'LL MEET A BEAUTIFUL GIRL AT CAMP, AND MAYBE WE'LL FALL IN LOVE AND BECOME CHILDHOOD SWEETHEARTS..

MAYBE I'LL SPEND THE WHOLE TWO WEEKS IN BED WITH POISON OAK!

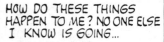

LUCY SAID YOU KNOW WHERE MY BIG BROTHER IS

WELL, I THINK I KNOW WHERE HE IS...

THEN GO FIND HIM!

SHALL I TELL HIM YOU'VE BEEN WORRIED ABOUT HIM?

NO, DON'T TELL HIM THAT! JUST FIND OUT IF HE'S EVER COMING HOME...

IF HE'S NOT COMING HOME, ASK HIM IF I CAN HAVE HIS LAMP AND DRESSER!!

I SORT OF FIGURED THAT YOU'D BE HERE, CHARLIE BROWN..

I TRIED TO GO TO CAMP... I REALLY DID... I WENT DOWN TO THE BUS STATION, BUT I JUST COULDN'T GET ON THE BUS...

THAT'S WHEN I CAME BACK HERE TO THE PITCHER'S MOUND... I'VE BEEN SITTING HERE FOR TWO DAYS... MAYBE I'LL SIT HERE FOR THE REST OF MY LIFE...

EVEN JOB GOT UP FROM AMONG THE ASHES EVENTUALLY..

JOB NEVER HAD TO WORRY ABOUT GOING TO SUMMER CAMP

THAT WAS A LONG FIRST ACT...DO YOU WANT TO WALK AROUND A BIT...MAYBE STRETCH OUR LEGS?

I COULD USE A DRINK OF WATER

The curtain of night enveloped the fleeing lovers.

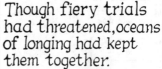

Though fiery trials had threatened, oceans of longing had kept them together.

Now, a new icicle of terror stabbed at the embroidery of their existence.

JOE METAPHOR!

DID YOU HAVE A GOOD TIME AT THE PARTY, BIG BROTHER?

FRANKLY, NO! I FELL INTO THE WADING POOL, AND EVERYBODY LAUGHED, AND THEN SOMEBODY SAID SOMETHING ABOUT HOW DUMB I WAS SO I CAME HOME...

I KNOW HOW YOU FEEL, BIG BROTHER...MAYBE YOU'D BE BETTER OFF IF YOU JUST STAYED HOME AND PLAYED WITH YOUR DOG...

I CAN'T EVEN DO THAT... HE'S STILL AT THE PARTY!

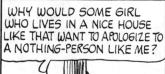

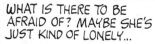

HERE'S THE WORLD-FAMOUS BEAGLE SCOUT LEADING HIS TROOP ON A NATURE HIKE...

AT THIS POINT, WE WILL SEPARATE... EACH WILL GO HIS OWN WAY...WE WILL MEET BACK HERE IN FORTY-FIVE MINUTES

THIS WILL TEACH AND PROMOTE SELF-RELIANCE

THAT WAS A SHORT FORTY-FIVE MINUTES!

JUST FOR THAT, WE'RE GOING TO TRY IT AGAIN !!!

AND I DON'T WANT TO SEE ANYONE HANGING AROUND MY FEET!

WAIT A MINUTE, PITCHER'!

DON'T START THE GAME UNTIL I GET MY SUNGLASSES ADJUSTED..

YOU THINK THAT'S GOING TO HELP?

YOU WOULDN'T WANT ME TO GET SUNBURNED TEETH, WOULD YOU?

SCHULZ

AND THEN I REMEMBER THAT TEST WE HAD IN HISTORY...

IT WAS EASY... I JUST GLANCED AT THE QUESTIONS AND BREEZED RIGHT THROUGH!

THAT MUST HAVE BEEN NICE

IN ALL MY LIFE, I'VE NEVER BREEZED RIGHT THROUGH!

SCHULZ

SALLY! YOUR BEACH BALL IS FLOATING AWAY!

IT'S GOING CLEAR ACROSS THE LAKE!

STAY CALM, BIG BROTHER...STAY CALM!

OKAY, YOU STUPID BEACH BALL, COME BACK HERE RIGHT NOW, OR I'LL SEE TO IT THAT YOU REGRET IT FOR THE REST OF YOUR LIFE!

YOU HAVE TO KNOW HOW TO TALK TO A BEACH BALL!

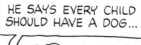

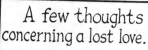
A few thoughts concerning a lost love.

Rats!

Z

RING!!

CLOMP!!

HOW DO YOU SET THE ALARM FOR A FLY BALL?

LOOK! I GOT AN AUTOGRAPHED BASEBALL FROM JOE SHLABOTNIK!

THIS IS THE BALL THAT JOE HIT WHEN HE GOT HIS BLOOP SINGLE IN THE NINTH INNING WITH HIS TEAM LEADING FIFTEEN TO THREE

AM I WRONG, OR DID HE MISSPELL HIS NAME?

HE DID, DIDN'T HE?

HE WAS PROBABLY EXCITED OVER HIS BLOOP SINGLE..

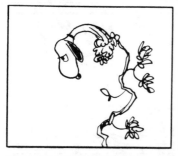

ANYONE WHO WOULD SIT IN A TREE PRETENDING TO BE A VULTURE SHOULD GO TO SEE A PSYCHIATRIST!

SHE'S SO STUPID...

SHE SHOULD KNOW THAT VULTURES ALMOST NEVER GO TO SEE PSYCHIATRISTS!

SCHULZ

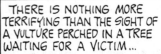
THERE IS NOTHING MORE TERRIFYING THAN THE SIGHT OF A VULTURE PERCHED IN A TREE WAITING FOR A VICTIM...

SIGH!

SUDDENLY, I JUST FELT VERY VERY RIDICULOUS!

SOMETIMES I THINK YOU MUST BE VERY NAÏVE

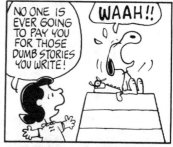
NO ONE IS EVER GOING TO PAY YOU FOR THOSE DUMB STORIES YOU WRITE!

WAAH!!

AND CRYING WON'T HELP... PUBLISHERS VERY SELDOM PAY AUTHORS JUST TO KEEP THEM FROM CRYING...

WHAT'S WRONG WITH THOSE GUYS?

HAVE YOU EVER BEEN IN A SITUATION WHERE YOU FELT YOU WERE IN OVER YOUR HEAD?

THAT'S HAPPENED TO ME A LOT LATELY...

AS SOON AS I GET UP IN THE MORNING, I FEEL I'M IN OVER MY HEAD!

WOODSTOCK IS THE ONLY PERSON I KNOW WHO COULD GET CHASED FOR THREE BLOCKS BY AN ABALONE!

AH!

.THIS IS GOING TO BE A GOOD DAY...

I GOT THE NEW CAN OF BALLS OPEN WITHOUT CUTTING MYSELF!

THIS IS A GREAT EXERCISE...

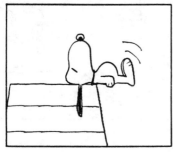

DO IT FIFTY TIMES A DAY, AND YOU'LL NEVER HAVE TO HAVE ACUPUNCTURE!

WATCH IT, DOG!

IF YOU TOUCH THAT BLANKET, THE ODDS ARE A THOUSAND TO ONE THAT YOU WILL END UP WITH A BROKEN ARM!

I ALWAYS GO WITH THE ODDS

Joe Sportscar spent ten thousand dollars on a new twelve cylinder Eloquent.

"You think more of that car than you do of me," complained his wife.

"All you ever do these days," she said, "is wax Eloquent!"

OH, WOW!!!! HOW DO I DO IT?!

DO YOU WANT TO HEAR SOME BASEBALL STATISTICS, CHARLIE BROWN?

ACCORDING TO MY FIGURES, AS OUR PITCHER, YOU HAD AN EARNED RUN AVERAGE THIS YEAR OF EIGHTY RUNS PER GAME!

STATISTICS DON'T LIE, CHARLIE BROWN

NO, BUT THEY SURE SHOOT OFF THEIR MOUTH A LOT!

AS OFFICIAL TEAM STATISTICIAN, I HAVE A FEW FIGURES TO REPORT..

DURING THIS PAST SEASON, WHILE YOU WERE IN RIGHT FIELD, NINETY-EIGHT FLY BALLS BOUNCED OVER YOUR HEAD...

SEVENTY-SIX GROUND BALLS ROLLED THROUGH YOUR LEGS AND YOU DROPPED TWO HUNDRED FLY BALLS...YOUR FIELDING AVERAGE FOR THE SEASON WAS .000

THE SUN WAS IN MY EYES!

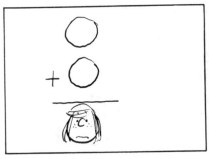

PLEASE DON'T SET YOUR LEMONADE ON MY PIANO...THE GLASS MIGHT LEAVE A RING...

OOOOOO!! AREN'T WE FUSSY, FUSSY, FUSSY?

KLUNK!

I'LL BET **BEETHOVEN** NEVER COMPLAINED WHEN A CUTE CHICK SET A GLASS OF LEMONADE ON **HIS** PIANO!!

"HOW MANY BARRELS IN A HOGSHEAD?"

"HOW MANY INCHES IN A NAIL? HOW MANY NAILS IN A QUARTER? HOW MANY SQUARE RODS IN A ROOD?"

HOW MANY WHATS IN A WHO? HOW MANY WHOS IN A WHAT?!

IT'S ZERO TIME!

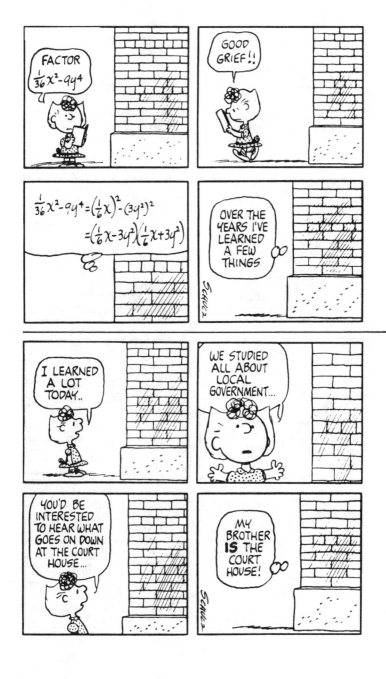

HA!

I GOT 'IM NOW!

TWO GOOD SERVES AND A COUPLE OF BAD CALLS, AND I'M IN!

TODAY IS VETERANS' DAY...

ON VETERANS' DAY I ALWAYS GO OVER TO BILL MAULDIN'S HOUSE AND QUAFF A FEW ROOT BEERS...

OL' BILL AND I HAVE LOTS IN COMMON... WE MADE T/3 AT THE SAME TIME...

AND WE WERE BOTH VERY CLOSE FRIENDS WITH GENERAL PATTON!

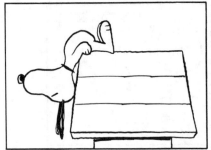

THIS IS THE GREAT NEW
EXERCISE I'VE DEVELOPED...

YOU HAVE TO DO THIS
FIFTY TIMES A DAY...

IT'S GOOD FOR
YOUR NECK...

AND YOUR BACK...

AND YOUR LEGS...

WUMP!

BUT IT RUINS
YOUR BODY...

HERE'S THE WORLD-FAMOUS BEAGLE SCOUT STARTING OFF ON A ROCK-HUNTING EXPEDITION..

AH! HERE'S A NICE ONE...

OOOO! HERE'S A BEAUTY!

AH!

THIS IS YOUR ROCK COLLECTION? LET ME SEE...

BOY, WHAT A DUMB-LOOKING ROCK COLLECTION! IT LOOKS LIKE YOU FOUND THEM ALL IN A DRIVEWAY!

NO ONE WOULD EVER BE INTERESTED IN A BUNCH OF ROCKS LIKE THAT..

NOT EVEN THEIR MOTHERS?

SCHULZ